New**Start** Hymns and Songs

the official

Churches Together Collection

for the Millennium and beyond

First published in Great Britain in 1999 by
KEVIN MAYHEW LIMITED
Buxhall
Stowmarket
Suffolk IP14 3DJ

The following editions are available

Words Only	ISBN	1 84003 326 6
	ISMN M	57004 566 2
	Catalogue No.	1413101
Full Music	ISBN	1 84003 327 4
	ISMN M	57004 522 8
	Catalogue No.	1413104

Cover design by Jaquetta Sergeant
Music setting by Donald Thomson
Printed and bound in Great Britain

Foreword

The Christian Churches of England have never worked so closely together on any major celebration as they have done for the Millennium celebration. A huge range of Christians – Catholics, Anglican, Nonconformist, Black Churches, New Churches – have come together to promote a New Start in this nation. A New Start is at the heart of the Gospel, and is the central message that the Churches have for the world as we enter the third Millennium.

So it is with very great pleasure that we commend to all of our Churches this supplement of new hymns and songs for worship. It deliberately draws from all the Christian traditions of worship represented in our Millennium celebrations. The editorial board was chosen to reflect all these traditions in their rich diversity, and has commissioned a collection which celebrates the New Start and the New Millennium. May this hymn book add to our understanding and our common worship as we enter the adventure of the third Millennium of our Lord.

Baroness Richardson
Bishop Crispian Hollis
Bishop Gavin Reid

Editorial Board

Introduction

At the heart of the Christian Gospel is the call to inclusiveness. No one is outside the embracing love of God who goes to the Cross for each one of us, and as Christ himself prayed for unity, we are called as Churches to model this inclusiveness.

So when a new collection of songs and hymns for the Millennium was proposed by the Churches' Millennium Group, it was clear that it had to reflect this inclusiveness. All Christian traditions would be invited to contribute, and the collection would be the first ever produced that was deliberately intended to reflect all these traditions.

The Millennium message of the Churches is simply the offer of a New Start – a New Start for the world's poor, a New Start at home, and a New Start with God. The Thematic Index is divided into these three headings so that worship can be planned around this Millennium message.

Putting this collection together has been an exciting project. The editorial board met only twice, and did much of its work at a distance. I am grateful to my colleagues for their help and advice, and to Kevin Mayhew and Jonathan Bugden for their gentle and patient guidance.

We offer this collection in a spirit of prayer, that it may enrich the worship of the Christian Churches at the start of a new Millennium of hope and inclusiveness.

The Revd Richard Thomas
Chairman, Editorial Board

The Millennium Resolution

Let there be
    respect for the earth
    peace for its people
    love in our lives
    delight in the good
    forgiveness for past wrongs
    and from now on a new start

1 Almighty God, we come to make confession

TUNE 1: DIVINE MERCY 11 10 11 10

1. Al - migh - ty God, we come to make con - fes - sion, for we have sinned in thought and word and deed. We now re - pent in hon - es - ty and sor - row; for - give us, Lord, and meet us in our need.

2. Forgiving God, I come to make confession
of all the harm and hurt that I have done;
of bitter words and many selfish actions,
forgive me, Lord, and make me like your Son.

3. Forgiving God, I come to make confession
of all that I have failed to do this day;
of help witheld, concern and love restricted,
forgive me, Lord, and lead me in your way.

4. Redeeming God, we come to seek forgiveness,
   for Jesus Christ has died to set us free.
   Forgive the past and fill us with your Spirit
   that we may live to serve you joyfully.

TUNE 2: FINLANDIA 10 10 10 10 10 10

1. Al - migh - ty God, we come to make con - fes - sion, for we have

sinned in thought and word and deed. We now re - pent in

hon - es - ty and sor - row; for - give us, Lord, and meet us in our

need. We now re - pent in hon - es - ty and sor - row;

for - give us, Lord, and meet us in our need.

Words: Christopher Ellis (b.1949)
Music: Tune 1 – Alan Rees (b.1941)
Tune 2 – Jean Sibelius (1865-1957)

2 At the heart of all things

TUNE 1: 67 67

1. At the heart of all things there is love, as Christ has shown. God of love, we praise you: heal-ing, bind-ing, mak-ing one. Puls-ing through cre-a-tion, life of God and life for all: love is in-vi-ta-tion, hu-man fu-ture, God's own call.

2. Love is kind and patient,
   never boastful, never rude;
   love can cope with all things,
   overcoming selfish mood.
   Trusting, hoping, loving:
   Jesus shows us how to care;
   love is still the best way,
   sign of life for all to share.

TUNE 2: LOVE INCARNATE 67 67

1. At the heart of all things there is love, as Christ has shown.

God of love, we praise you: heal - ing, bind - ing, mak - ing one.

2. Pulsing through creation,
   life of God and life for all:
   love is invitation,
   human future, God's own call.

3. Love is kind and patient,
   never boastful, never rude;
   love can cope with all things,
   overcoming selfish mood.

4. Trusting, hoping, loving:
   Jesus shows us how to care;
   love is still the best way,
   sign of life for all to share.

Words, based on 1 Corinthians 13: Christopher Ellis (b.1949)
Music: Tune 1 – Rodney Bambrick (b.1927)
Tune 2 – C. E. Pettman (1865-1943)

3 Beyond the fringes of the church

2. Beyond the fringes of the church,
   but not beyond the love of God,
   are thousands more who do not know
   the joy we celebrate today.
   Teach us to demonstrate your truth
   in ways their culture understands;
   and make us bold to speak of you,
   and point them all to Christ the Living Way.

Words and Music: Brian Hoare (b.1935)

4 Birth brings a promise

TUNE 1: NEWBORN 11 10 11 10

1. Birth brings a promise of new life awaking, dawning of hope through a child's open eyes. Uncharted future is there for the making, challenge and change in a baby's first cries.

2. Ev'ry new life changes those who are round it
making demands of commitment and care,
calling for love to enfold and surround it,
reshaping patterns by claiming a share.

3. Jesus, the new-born, crossed time's moving stages
changing their course by the act of his birth,
translating God from the mystery of ages,
rooting our faith by his presence on earth.

4. Wonder and worship were waiting to greet him,
love and devotion were his to command,
life was transformed for the ones sent to meet him,
touching their God in a child's outstretched hand.

5. Birth gives a promise of new life awaking.
Jesus, the new-born, calls us to new birth.
All that he promised is ours for the taking
when our commitment brings God down to earth.

TUNE 2: EPIPHANY 11 10 11 10

1. Birth brings a pro-mise of new life a-wak - ing,
dawn - ing of hope through a child's o - pen eyes.
Un - chart - ed fu - ture is there for the mak - ing,
chal - lenge and change in a ba - by's first cries.

Words: Marjorie Dobson (b.1940)
Music: Tune 1 – Basil E. Bridge (b.1927)
Tune 2 – J. F. Thrupp (1827-1867)

5 Blessing and honour

serve your will; you fill the hea-vens,

earth shows your glo-ry, and just and true are all your ways!

2. Jesus, our Saviour,
   you left the heavens,
   and came to earth
   in human form;
   humbly obedient,
   you died to save us,
   but now you live
   as Lord of all!

3. O Holy Spirit,
   breath of the Father,
   poured out on all
   to make us new;
   life-giving Spirit,
   fountain of goodness,
   you fill your church
   with love and power!

Words and Music: Brian Hoare (b.1935)

6 Bright, bright, the shining of Christ's saving way

MYERSCOUGH 10 9 12 9

1. Bright, bright, the shin-ing of Christ's sav - ing way.

E - ver new, the time-less Eas - ter day, whose

life - giv-ing light search-es deep, makes all things whole.

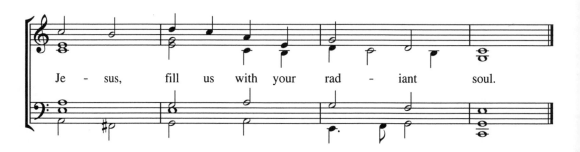

Je - sus, fill us with your rad - iant soul.

2. Deep, deep the anguish of this broken world.
   Torn with sorrow streams our joy unfurled –
   a joy in the beauty of this so fragile earth,
   Jesus, life affirm; inspire new birth.

3. Brave, brave the voices that protesting cry –
   cry for justice and humanity.
   Cast out on the edge, on the margin, life denied,
   Jesus, show to us your wounded side.

4. Far, far the galaxies extend their scope.
   Vast our wonder, yet profound our hope.
   Our world has evolved through unfathomable grace.
   Jesus, bond in peace this sacred place.

5. Call, call us onward; let the scene unfold.
   Time's deep fountain flows to form and mould.
   Your word is our rock; holy wisdom is our guide.
   Jesus, be our star amid the tide.

6. Change, change is all around; the prospect new.
   Grace transforming re-creates the view.
   The old order fades; fresh perspectives greet the sight.
   Jesus, ever be our Way, our Light.

Words and Music: John Aspinwall (b.1931)

7 But when the time had fully come

TUNE 1: THURLESTONE 87 88 7

1. But when the time had ful-ly come, the time by God ap-point-ed, when all the past would be ful-filled, there came a-mong us, as God willed, the Christ, the Lord's a-noint-ed.

2. But when the time had fully come
   how few had recognised him!
   They never dreamt God's Son could be
   that carpenter from Galilee;
   their lack of faith surprised him.

3. But when the time had fully come
   his close companions failed him;
   then, handed over by a friend,
   both church and state conspired his end;
   upon a cross they nailed him.

4. But when the time had fully come
   not evil's worst endeavour
   could hold him in the tomb; the hour
   of hope fulfilled had dawned; the power
   of love holds good for ever.

TUNE 2: LUTHER'S HYMN 87 88 7

1. But when the time had ful - ly come, the time by God ap -
point - ed, when all the past would be ful - filled, there
came a - mong us, as God willed, the Christ, the Lord's a - noint - ed.

Words, based on Galatians 4:4: Basil E. Bridge (b.1927)
Music: Tune 1 – Malcolm McKelvey (b.1926)
Tune 2 – from 'Geistliche Lieder', Wittenberg (1535)

8 Celebrate the faith together

2. What we know we declare:
news to tell, Christ to share.
Spread the Word, name the Name:
this is the gospel that we proclaim.

Words and Music: Brian Hoare (b.1935)

9 Christ brings the kingdom

TUNE 1: GASQUET HALL 10 10 10 10

2. Come to his kingdom of weakness made strong,
   brokenness mended, the blind given sight;
   welcome and dignity crown the despised,
   darkness is banished by glorious light.

3. Come to his kingdom where righteousness reigns –
   God has commanded: repent and believe!
   Children of dust in his glory may share,
   penitent rebels his favour receive.

4. Come to his kingdom of laughter and hope,
   savour the freedom its fullness will bring:
   no more oppression, injustice or fear –
   come to the kingdom where Jesus is King!

TUNE 2: SLANE 10 10 10 10

1. Christ brings the king - dom where bar - ren - ness blooms:

see how the im - age of God is res - tored,

yield - ing a har - vest of tal - ents and skills

when we ac - know - ledge our Mak - er as Lord.

Words, based on Isaiah 35: 1, 3, 8, 10: Martin E. Leckebusch (b.1962)
Music: Tune 1 – Christopher Tambling (b.1964)
Tune 2 – traditional Irish melody arr. Colin Hand (b.1929)

10 Christian people, sing together

TUNE 1: BIRCH GREEN 87 87D

2. God created countless faces,
   yet in Christ we all are one.
   Though we look from many angles,
   all our views reflect the Son.
   So we bring each gift and talent,
   off'ring what we have to share,
   and God blends us all together
   in one body of his care.

3. Teach us, Lord, to trust each other,
   though our ways are not the same.
   As you call us to your purpose,
   bless our working in your name.
   In the world of daily living
   each uniquely serves your will,
   show how ev'ry person matters,
   as our calling we fulfil.

A lower setting of Tune 2 will be found at No. 56

TUNE 2: ODE TO JOY 87 87D

1. Christ-ian peo-ple, sing to-geth-er, all un-i-ted in one voice.

Though we come from ma-ny cul-tures, yet in Christ we all re-joice.

In our dai-ly lives we're scat-tered, serv-ing God in var-ious ways.

Then in wor-ship we're un-i-ted, giv-ing him our thanks and praise.

Words: Marjorie Dobson (b.1940)
Music: Tune 1 – Brian Hoare (b.1935)
Tune 2 – Ludwig van Beethoven (1770-1827) arr. Christopher Tambling (b.1964)

11 Come and join the great uprising

MARCHING THROUGH GEORGIA 13 13 13 8 and Refrain

joice! Re - joice! Death's reign of fear has ceased.

E - vil is de - feat - ed by the Prince of love and peace,

this is the world's new be - gin - ning.

2. Jesus has defeated all manipulative powers,
   proven the futility of fortresses and towers;
   victims of oppression share the triumph of this hour:
   this is the world's new beginning.

3. Life in all its fullness is his gift for us to share:
   wholeness and security for people everywhere.
   Dare we live his life, to make creation just and fair?
   This is the world's new beginning.

4. Share the resurrection hope and put an end to fear,
   sorrow turns to joy and life eternal starts right here!
   Heav'n and earth unite to give a great resounding cheer!
   This is the world's new beginning.

Words: Michael Forster (b.1946)
Music: Henry Clay Work (1832-1884) arr. Donald Thomson (b.1968)

12 Come, wounded healer

TUNE 1: DEEPCAR 10 11 11 11

1. Come, wound-ed heal-er, your suff-'rings re-veal – the scars you ac-cep-ted, our an-guish to heal. Your wounds bring such com-fort in bo-dy and soul to all who bear tor-ment and yearn to be whole.

2. Come, hated Lover, and gather us near,
   your welcome, your teaching, your challenge to hear:
   where scorn and abuse cause rejection and pain,
   your loving acceptance makes hope live again!

3. Come, broken Victor, condemned to a cross –
   how great are the treasures we gain from your loss!
   Your willing agreement to share in our strife
   transforms our despair into fullness of life.

TUNE 2: SLANE 10 11 11 11

1. Come, wound-ed heal-er, your suff-'rings re-veal – the scars you ac-cep-ted, our an-guish to heal. Your wounds bring such com-fort in bo-dy and soul to all who bear tor-ment and yearn to be whole.

Words: Martin E. Leckebusch (b.1962)
Music: Tune 1 – Richard Lloyd (b.1933)
Tune 2 – traditional Irish melody arr. Colin Hand (b.1929)

13 Creating God, we bring our song of praise

TUNE 1: AD LIMINA 10 10 10 10

Unison

1. Cre-at-ing God, we bring our song of praise for life and work that ce-le-brate your ways: the skill of hands, our liv-ing with the earth, the joy that comes from know-ing our own worth.

2. Forgiving God, we bring our cries of pain
   for all that shames us in our search for gain:
   the hidden wounds, the angry scars of strife,
   the emptiness that saps and weakens life.

3. Redeeming God, we bring our trust in you,
   our fragile hope that all may be made new:
   our dreams of truth, of wealth that all may share,
   of work and service rooted deep in prayer.

4. Renewing God, we offer what shall be
   a world that lives and works in harmony:
   when peace and justice, once so long denied,
   restore to all their dignity and pride.

TUNE 2: WOODLANDS 10 10 10 10

Unison

1. Cre - at - ing God, we bring our song of praise for life and work that ce - le - brate your ways: the skill of hands, our liv - ing with the earth, the joy that comes from know - ing our own worth.

Words: Jan Berry (b.1953)
Music: Tune 1 – Andrew Moore (b.1954)
Tune 2 – Walter Greatorex (1877-1949)

14 Creation is awaiting

1. Cre - a -tion is a-wait-ing the re - turn of the King. The trees are poised to clap their hands for joy. The moun-tains stand ma-jes - tic to sal - ute their God; the des - ert lies in wait to burst in - to bloom. The King is com - ing, the King is

2. The church is awaiting the return of the King.
   The people joined together in his love.
   Redeemed by his blood,
   washed in his word.
   As a bride longs for her bridegroom
   the Church looks to God.

   The King is coming,
   the King is coming,
   the King is coming to receive his bride.

3. The world is awaiting the return of the King.
   The earth is a footstool for his feet.
   Every knee will bow down,
   every tongue confess,
   that Jesus Christ is Lord
   of heaven and earth.

   The King is coming,
   the King is coming,
   the King is coming to reign in majesty.

Words and Music: Chris Bowater (b.1947) and Ian Taylor (b.1957)

15 Dance in your Spirit

free now to sing, free to dance and shout,

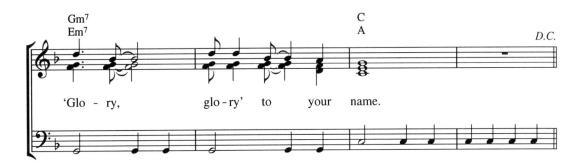

'Glo - ry, glo - ry' to your name.

D.C.

2. Jesus, you opened your arms for us,
   but we nailed them to the cross;
   but you are risen and now we live,
   free from, free from ev'ry fear.

3. Your Spirit brings peace and gentleness,
   kindness, self-control and love,
   patience and goodness and faith and joy,
   Spirit, Spirit fill us now.

Words and Music: Mike Anderson (b.1956)

New**Start** Hymns and Songs

16 Deep within the shadow of your wings

Unison

1. Deep with-in the sha-dow of your wings I will rest, I will stay.

Rea-dy as the eag-le to a-rise I will wait in you, O my Lord.

2. Growing in the vineyard of your care
I will rest,
I will stay.
Grafted as a branch upon the vine
bearing fruit for you,
O my Lord.

3. Hidden in the quiver of your love
I will rest,
I will stay.
Ready as your arrow to be sent
to a waiting world,
O my Lord.

Words: Catherine Williams (b.1965)
Music: Norman Warren (b.1934)

17 Every fiftieth year
Jubilee

JUBILEE 10 10 11 11

1. Ev-'ry fif-tieth year set the cap-tives free: let a trum-pet blast, sum-mon ju-bi-lee. And God bless the peo-ple, the poor, tired and torn; for it's in their lives that love must be re-born.

1.- 3. D.C.

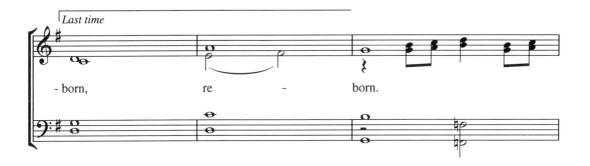

Last time

- born, re - born.

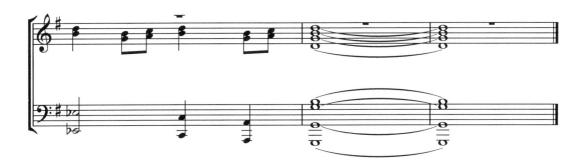

2. Let the earth find rest
   where no rest is known:
   give the world's oppressed
   what should be their own.

   And God bless the people,
   the poor, tired and torn;
   for it's in their lives
   that love must be reborn.

3. Cancel every debt,
   terminate all fraud;
   let the use of wealth
   serve the cause of God.

   And God bless. . .

4. Let the hills resound,
   let the oceans roar,
   celebrate the good,
   heaven and earth restore.

   And God bless the people,
   the poor, tired and torn;
   for it's in their lives
   that love must be reborn, reborn.

Words and Music: John L. Bell (b.1949) and Graham Maule (b.1958)

18 First light

first note of the free - dom song,   first breath of the
first light is the ris - en one,   first born o - ver
first light is the ris - en Son,   the first and the

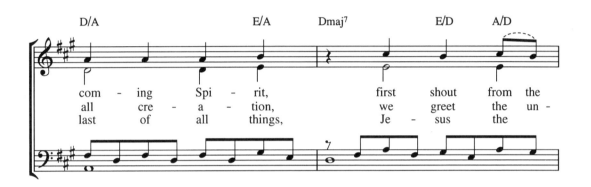

com - ing Spi - rit,   first shout from the
all cre - a - tion,   we greet the un -
last of all things,   Je - sus the

To next verse

con - quered tomb.
con - quered Son.
Light has

Last time

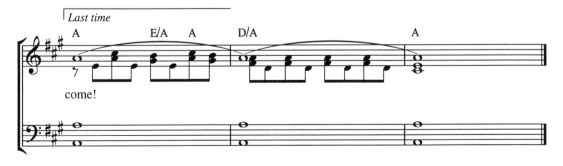

come!

Words: Graham Kendrick (b.1950)
Music: Graham Kendrick (b.1950) arr. Donald Thomson (b.1968)

19 God made a boomerang

With bounce

Refrain

Unison

God made a boom - er - ang and called it love,

God made a boom - er - ang and called it love,

God made a boom - er - ang and called it love, and

then he threw it a - way!

1. Love's like a boom - er - ang, that's what we've found, it

2. Love's like a boomerang, that's what God planned,
   but it's no use if it stays in your hand.
   Gotta send it spinning
   for a new beginning,
   love's like a boomerang, let's throw it around.

3. Love's like a boomerang, goes with a swing,
   now ev'rybody can have a good fling.
   Families and nations
   join the celebrations,
   love's like a boomerang, let's throw it around.

Words: Michael Forster (b.1946)
Music: Christopher Tambling (b.1964)

New**Start** Hymns and Songs

20 God of all human history

CALLOW END 77 77 77

1. God of all hu-man his-tory, of time long fled and fad-ed, yours is the sec-ret mas-tery by which the years are guid-ed: King of un-chang-ing glo-ry from a-ges un-re-cord-ed.

2. God of the hidden future
   unfolding life for ever,
   hope of each ransomed creature
   as time speeds ever faster:
   raise us to our full stature
   in Christ, our one Redeemer.

3. God of this present moment
   requiring our decision,
   now is the hour of judgement
   for ruin or salvation:
   give us complete commitment
   to your most urgent mission.

Words: Christopher Idle (b.1938)
Music: Alan Rees (b.1941)

21 God of every changing season

TUNE 1: HOPE PARK 87 87 D

1. God of ev - 'ry chang - ing sea - son, in - ner worlds and ou - ter space, still be - yond the grasp of rea - son, yield - ing still to love's em - brace, we, your peo - ple, make thanks - giv - ing, bridg - ing cul - ture, lan - guage, race, for the faith that Christ is liv - ing, for two thou - sand years of grace.

2. When, in savage mock-enthronement,
   Jesus died on Calvary,
   then was made a real atonement,
   rooted deep in history.
   Partners now in new creation,
   sharing all its joy and pain,
   pierced with glad anticipation,
   we await his final reign.

3. God, as Holy Spirit working,
   help us meanwhile find and clear
   all the mines of hatred lurking
   in the no-man's-land of fear.
   Do not let us worship money,
   lost in deserts made by greed,
   while your land of milk and honey
   waits to satisfy our need.

4. In the world's ongoing story
   now a new page open lies.
   Print it, Lord, with grace and glory,
   read it with our Saviour's eyes.
   Through all trials keep before us
   symbols faith will recognise,
   cross and crown, to reassure us
   God, our source, is God, our prize.

TUNE 2: AUSTRIA 87 87 D

1. God of ev-'ry chang-ing sea-son, in-ner worlds and ou-ter space,

still be-yond the grasp of rea-son, yield-ing still to love's em-brace,

we, your peo-ple, make thanks-giv-ing, bridg-ing cul-ture, lan-guage, race,

for the faith that Christ is liv-ing, for two thou-sand years of grace.

Words: Elizabeth Cosnett (b.1936)
Music: Tune 1 – Ian Sharp (b.1943)
Tune 2 – Croation folk melody adapted by Franz Joseph Haydn (1732-1809)

22 God of love

TUNE 1: SCHUMANN 87 87 D

1. God of love, you free-ly give us bles-sings more than we de-serve;
be our light in times of dark-ness, be our strength when fears un-nerve.
In this age when proof con-vin-ces, help us see where wis-dom lies;
more en-dur-ing than per-sua-sion is your truth which ne-ver dies.

2. Son incarnate, yours the presence
which can heal an aching heart;
over death you reign triumphant,
you alone new life impart.
From your birth so long awaited,
to the cross on Calvary,
you will serve as our example,
let us, Lord, your servants be.

3. Holy Spirit, inspiration,
   day by day, yet mystery;
   with the Son and the Creator
   you form mystic unity.
   Draw us into your communion,
   with the love that sets us free;
   bind our hearts to you for ever,
   holy, blessèd Trinity.

TUNE 2: EVERTON 87 87 D

1. God of love, you free-ly give us bles-sings more than we de-serve; be our light in times of dark-ness, be our strength when fears un-nerve. In this age when proof con-vin-ces, help us see where wis-dom lies; more en-dur-ing than per-sua-sion is your truth which ne-ver dies.

Words: Jean Holloway (b.1939)
Music: Tune 1 – Robert Schumann (1810-1856) adapted and arranged by Richard Lloyd (b.1933)
Tune 2 – Henry Smart (1813-1879)

23 God of mission, still you send us

TUNE 1: ALFOXTON 87 87 87

1. God of mis - sion, still you send us to a world that needs your grace. You have gone a - head to meet us, you are wait - ing in each place. Show us now your lov - ing glo - ry in each child of ev - 'ry race.

2. God of hope, you call your people
   to become the future now!
   Help us see your will more clearly,
   grant us visions, show us how
   in your strength, despite our weakness,
   we might live your kingdom now.

3. You have called us to be partners
   in the mission of your Son.
   Black and white and male and female,
   you have called us to be one.
   Teach us how to serve together
   that through us your will be done.

TUNE 2: RHUDDLAN 87 87 87

1. God of mis - sion, still you send us to a world that

needs your grace. You have gone a - head to meet us,

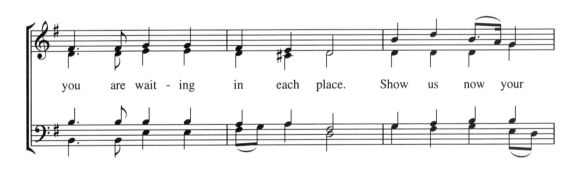

you are wait - ing in each place. Show us now your

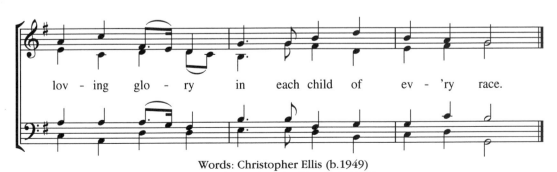

lov - ing glo - ry in each child of ev - 'ry race.

Words: Christopher Ellis (b.1949)
Music: Tune 1 – John Marsh (b.1939)
Tune 2 – traditional Welsh melody from 'Musical Relicks of Welsh Bards' (1800)

24 God of the passing centuries

GONFALON ROYAL LM

Let there be
1. God of the pas - sing cen - tu - ries,
of time com - ple - ted and to come: we
bring our pray'r that you will make our long - ing and our
liv - ing one. A - men.

respect for the earth 2. Give us the wisdom, purpose, strength,
to cherish all your hand has made,
peace for its people   that ev'ry nation, ev'ry child,
may live in peace, be unafraid.

love in our lives

3. We seek, for living fuller lives,
   with stranger, neighbour, loved one, friend,
   the love which you intend for all,
   which finds in Christ its source and end.

delight in the good

4. To all that brings delight in life,
   moments of vision, joyful days,
   all that has shaped us, leads us on,
   we say our 'Yes' with thanks and praise.

forgiveness for past wrong

5. God of forgiveness, set us free
   from suffered and inflicted pain,
   heal us from hatred born of fear,
   empower us all for life again.

and from now on a new start

6. That with the turning of the year,
   renewed in hope and glad of heart,
   safe in the knowledge of your grace,
   we may from now, make a new start.

Words: Peter Trow (b.1956)
Music: Percy Carter Buck (1871-1947)

25 God whose love is everywhere
Christingle Hymn

FALLING FIFTHS 77 75 77 5
The orange, representing all the world.

1. God whose love is ev - 'ry - where made our earth and

all things fair, e - ver keeps them in his care,

praise the God of love! He who hung the stars in space

holds the spin - ning world in place; praise the

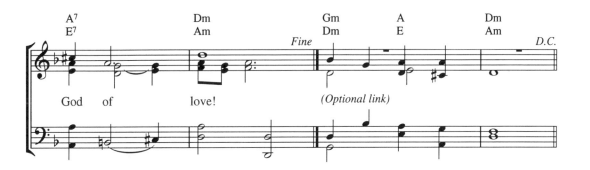

God of love!   *(Optional link)*

*The sticks,
fruit and nuts,
representing
the four
seasons and
the fruit of
the earth.*

2. Come with thankful songs to sing
   of the gifts the seasons bring,
   summer, winter, autumn, spring;
   praise the God of love!
   He who gave us breath and birth
   gives us all the fruitful earth;
   praise the God of love!

*The red
ribbon,
representing
the blood of
Christ shed
for us.*

3. Mark what love the Lord displayed,
   all our sins upon him laid,
   by his blood our ransom paid;
   praise the God of love!
   Circled by that scarlet band
   all the world is in his hand;
   praise the God of love!

*The lighted
candle,
representing
Christ
the Light of
the world.*

4. See the sign of love appear,
   flame of glory, bright and clear,
   light for all the world is here;
   praise the God of love!
   Gloom and darkness, get you gone!
   Christ the Light of life has shone;
   praise the God of love!

Words: Timothy Dudley-Smith (b.1926)
Music: Noël Tredinnick (b.1949)

26 Gracious God, in adoration

TUNE 1: GOULDSBROOK 87 87 87

1. Gra - cious God, in a - do - ra - tion saints with joy be - fore you fall; on - ly when our hearts are lead - en can we fail to hear their call: 'Come with won - der, serve with glad - ness God whose pow'r cre - a - ted all.'

2. Earth and sky in silent praises
   speak to those with eyes to see;
   all earth's living creatures echo
   'God has made us!' So may we
   come with wonder, serve with gladness
   him through whom they came to be.

3. You have made us in your image,
   breathed your Spirit, given us birth;
   Jesus calls, whose cross has given
   ev'ry life eternal worth,
   'Come with wonder, serve with gladness,
   let God's will be done on earth!'

4. Earth by war and want is threatened;
   deep the roots of fear and greed;
   let your mercy be our measure
   as we see our neighbour's need,
   come with wonder, serve with gladness,
   share your gift of daily bread.

5. Holy Spirit, urging, striving,
   give us love that casts out fear,
   courage, seeking peace with justice,
   faith to make this message clear –
   'Come with wonder, serve with gladness,
   live in hope; the Lord is near!'

TUNE 2: REGENT SQUARE 87 87 87

1. Gra - cious God, in a - do - ra - tion saints with joy be - fore you fall; on - ly when our hearts are lead - en can we fail to hear their call: 'Come with won - der, serve with glad - ness God whose pow'r cre - a - ted all.'

Words: Basil Bridge (b.1927)
Music: Tune 1 – Malcolm Archer (b.1952)
Tune 2 – Henry Smart (1813-1879)

27 Great is the power we proclaim

of the Lord. Gifts of the Spi-rit for us to in-he-rit, to build up the Bo-dy of Christ.

D.C.

2. God's people called to bring
   to the world the peace of Christ.
   Love for our neighbour,
   and justice in our labour,
   compelled by the love of Christ.

3. God's people called to pray
   for the Church to be made one.
   One holy nation
   in hope of salvation,
   brothers and sisters in Christ.

4. God's people called today
   to make known the love of God.
   Seeds we are sowing
   with faith that is growing
   strong in the power of Christ.

5. God's people called to share
   in the blessing cup of Christ:
   bread that is broken,
   and Word that is spoken,
   one in the Body of Christ.

Words and Music: Christopher Walker (b.1947)

28 Here on the threshold of a new beginning

ADVENIT 11 10 11 10 D

1. Here on the thres-hold of a new beg-in-ning,
by grace for-gi-ven, now we leave be-hind
our long-re-pen-ted sel-fish-ness and sin-ning,
and all our bles-sings call a-gain to mind:
Christ to re-deem us, ran-som and re-store us,

the love that holds us in a Sa-viour's care,

faith strong to wel - come all that lies be - fore us,

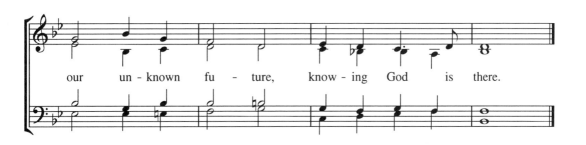

our un-known fu - ture, know-ing God is there.

2. May we, your children, feel with Christ's compassion
an earth disordered, hungry and in pain;
then, at your calling, find the will to fashion
new ways where freedom, truth and justice reign;
where wars are ended, ancient wrongs are righted,
and nations value human life and worth;
where in the darkness lamps of hope are lighted
and Christ is honoured over all the earth.

3. So may your wisdom shine from scripture's pages
to mould and make us stones with which to build
God's holy temple, through eternal ages,
one church united, strong and Spirit-filled;
heirs to the fullness of your new creation
in faith we follow, pledged to be your own;
yours is the future, ours the celebration,
for Christ is risen! God is on the throne!

Words: Timothy Dudley-Smith (b.1926)
Music: Malcolm Archer (b.1952)

29 If my people, who are called by my name

2. We, your people, who are called by your name,
will humble ourselves and pray.
We, your people, will seek your face,
and turn from our wicked ways.
O Father, hear from heaven and forgive us.
O Father, hear from heav'n and heal our land.
Your eyes are open and your ears are list'ning
as your people hear and understand.

Words: Geoff Baker (b.1958)
Music: Geoff Baker (b.1958) arr. Donald Thomson (b.1968)

30 I hear somebody calling

TUNE 1: POPLE'S WELL 13 13 13 13

1. I hear some-bo-dy call-ing, a voice from far a-way; it's cry-ing out for jus-tice, and yearn-ing for that day when no-one need go hun-gry, des-pair will be no more – a day which glad-ly he-ralds a new start for the poor.

To next verse

Last time

2. I hear somebody calling, a voice from somewhere near;
it's crying out with longing, yet no one seems to hear.
Despite long years of witness, a multitude still search –
forgive us, Lord, and grant now a new start for the church.

3. I hear somebody calling, a voice from all around;
it's crying out in anguish, the grim and tragic sound
of God's creation groaning, stripped bare, denied her worth –
Lord, curb our greed, and bring now a new start for the earth.

4. I hear somebody calling, a voice from close at hand;
   it's crying out in anger, campaigning for a land
   where all will be respected, and war will find no place –
   a world of peace and friendship, a new start for our race.

5. I hear somebody calling, a voice from deep within;
   it's crying out for mercy, confessing all my sin.
   Lord come to me, I beg you, for I have lost my way –
   reach out in love and grant now a new start for today.

6. I hear somebody calling, a voice from far above;
   it's crying out in sorrow, and urging us to love,
   for still a world lies bleeding, the weak go to the wall –
   God grant in your great mercy a new start for us all.

TUNE 2: BRADFIELD 13 13 13 13

Words: Nick Fawcett (b.1957)
Music: Tune 1 – Malcolm Archer (b.1952)
Tune 2 – Richard Lloyd (b.1933)

31 In an age of twisted values
Heal our nation

TUNE 1: KILVE 87 87 D

1. In an age of twis-ted val - ues we have lost the truth we
need; in so - phi - sti - ca-ted lan - guage we have jus - ti - fied our
greed; by our strug - gle for pos - ses - sions we have robbed the poor and
weak – hear our cry and heal our na - tion: your for- give - ness, Lord, we seek.

2. We have built discrimination
   on our prejudice and fear;
   hatred swiftly turns to cruelty
   if we hold resentments dear.
   For communities divided
   by the walls of class and race
   hear our cry and heal our nation:
   show us, Lord, your love and grace.

3. When our families are broken;
   when our homes are full of strife;
   when our children are bewildered,
   when they lose their way in life;
   when we fail to give the aged
   all the care we know we should –
   hear our cry and heal our nation
   with your tender fatherhood.

4. We who hear your word so often
    choose so rarely to obey;
    turn us from our wilful blindness,
    give us truth to light our way.
    In the power of your Spirit
    come to cleanse us, make us new:
    hear our cry and heal our nation
    till our nation honours you.

TUNE 2: CALON LÂN 87 87 D

1. In an age of twis-ted val – ues we have lost the truth we need; in so-phi-sti-ca-ted lan – guage we have jus – ti-fied our greed; by our strug – gle for pos-ses – sions we have robbed the poor and weak – hear our cry and heal our na – tion: your for-give – ness, Lord, we seek.

Words: Martin E. Leckebusch (b.1962)
Music: Tune 1 – John Marsh (b.1939)
Tune 2 – John Hughes (1872-1914)

32 In the silence of the Godhead
From eternity to eternity

BARLOW 87 87 876

Unison

1. In the si - lence of the God- head there is born the Fa - ther's Word, God from God and light e - ter-nal, his be - lov'd and on - ly Son; in their rap - ture of com - mu - nion breathes the Spi - rit of their love, one God in Tri - ni - ty.

2. Through his Word the gracious Father
   bids the world in splendour rise;
   man and woman in God's image
   bear the imprint of his love;
   to their care is now entrusted
   all the beauty of the earth,
   one world in harmony.

3. When they turn from their Creator
   God in mercy sends his Son;
   he will take our human nature
   to redeem the world from sin,
   to restore love's broken image
   in the hearts that love has made,
   in love that knows no end.

4. In the silence of Good Friday
   all the world in darkness lies,
   for the light of all the ages
   in the sleep of death is found;
   but the seed of God's great harvest
   waits to rise at God's command,
   the living Word of God.

5. In the dawn of Easter Sunday
   death and sin are overcome;
   Christ, the Lord of life, is risen,
   glorious firstborn from the dead;
   in this springtime of creation
   Christ has made the world anew
   in love and unity.

6. Glory be to God the Father,
   fount from whom all blessings flow;
   glory be to God, our Saviour,
   King of kings, and Lord of lords;
   glory be to God the Spirit,
   bond of love in unity,
   one God in Trinity.

Words: James Quinn (b.1919)
Music: Christopher Tambling (b.1964)

New**Start** Hymns and Songs

33 I saw the wind in the sky

MYSTERY 78 75 75

Unison

1. I saw the wind in the sky, the spar-kle of fire in the dew, dance of a child in the sand, the steps of the old. Give me your eyes, liv-ing Lord, for lov-ing to-day.

2. I felt the breeze in my hair,
   the warmth of the sun in my heart;
   I felt the presence of joy,
   the touch of a hand.
   Make me aware, living Lord,
   for loving today.

3. I heard the flight of the gulls,
   the boom of the sea in the caves,
   groaning of rocks in the earth,
   a cry from the heart.
   Give me your ears, living Lord,
   for loving today.

4. I know the pulse of my blood,
   the freshness of life in my breath,
   I sense the source of my soul,
   the well-spring divine.
   Give me your power, living Lord,
   for loving today.

5. I know the darkness of sin,
   the blight of my guilt and despair,
   I know the coming of love,
   the lifting of heart.
   Give me your grace, living Lord,
   for loving today.

6. I have a pathway to tread,
   a place at the table to fill;
   destiny shaped by your hands,
   a vision of joy.
   Give me yourself, living Lord,
   for loving today.

Words: David Bartleet (b.1929)
Music: Norman Warren (b.1934)

34 Jesus, in the new dawn

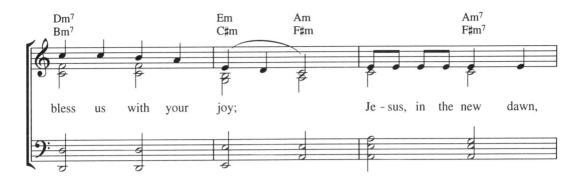

Dm⁷ / Bm⁷				Em / C♯m	Am / F♯m				Am⁷ / F♯m⁷	

bless   us   with   your   joy;   Je - sus, in the new dawn,

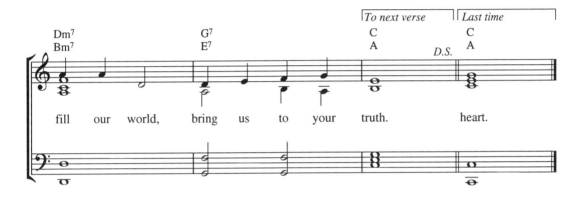

To next verse | *Last time*

Dm⁷ / Bm⁷		G⁷ / E⁷				C / A		C / A

D.S.

fill   our   world,   bring   us   to   your   truth.   heart.

2. Spirit, in the new dawn, sing to us,
    play for us your song;
    Spirit, in the new dawn, sing to us,
    we will join your dance;
    Spirit, in the new dawn, take our hearts,
    birth in us your peace;
    Spirit, in the new dawn, take our hearts,
    make them one with yours.

3. Father, in the new dawn, speak to us,
    plant in us your love;
    Father, in the new dawn, speak to us,
    teach us to forgive;
    Father, in the new dawn, hold us fast,
    bring us to new life;
    Father, in the new dawn, hold us fast,
    bind us to your heart.

Words and Music: Margaret Rizza (b.1929)

35 Jesus, in your life we see you

TUNE 1: BOLSTERSTONE 87 87 D

1. Je - sus, in your life we see you mak - ing God's com - pas - sion known, 'Sure - ly you have borne our sor - rows, sure - ly made our pain your own!' see your touch bring hope and heal - ing, see your word set cap - tives free, see you suf - fer, mocked, re - jec - ted, dy - ing on the shame - ful tree.

2. Risen Lord, you reign in glory;
   but your wounded hands still show
   you can share the outcast's torment,
   sound the depths of human woe,
   know where greed exploits the helpless,
   hear the addict's lonely cry,
   grieve at so much waste and heartbreak,
   feel for all who question 'why?'

3. Risen Lord, you bear their sorrow,
   know how much they need your peace;
   as you once healed broken bodies,
   offered captive souls release,
   take us, use us in your service;
   we would follow where you lead;
   only your divine compassion
   meets the depths of human need.

TUNE 2: BLAENWERN 87 87 D

1. Je - sus, in your life we see you mak - ing God's com -
pas - sion known, 'Sure - ly you have borne our sor - rows,
sure - ly made our pain your own!' see your touch bring
hope and heal - ing, see your word set cap - tives free, see you
suf - fer, mocked, re - jec - ted, dy - ing on the shame - ful tree.

Words: Basil E. Bridge (b.1927)
Music: Tune 1 – Richard Lloyd (b.1933)
Tune 2 – William Penfro Rowlands (1860-1937)

36 Jesus, the broken bread

TUNE 1: HESWALL 10 10 10 10

1. Je - sus, the bro - ken bread, we come to you;
emp - ty, we would be fed – meet us a - new.
Teach us to hun - ger af - ter right - eous - ness,
reach out in love, we pray, to guide and bless.

2. Jesus, the poured out wine, we come with awe;
thirsty, we take the cup – quench and restore.
Teach us to seek your kingdom and your will,
reach out in love, we pray, our lives to fill.

3. Jesus, the crucified, we come with shame;
greedy, we've sought reward – made that our aim.
Teach us to worship now through word and deed,
reach out in love, we pray, to all in need.

4. Jesus, the risen Lord, we come with praise;
   gladly, we sing of you, our hearts ablaze.
   Teach us to glimpse new life beyond the grave,
   reach out in love, we pray, to heal and save.

5. Jesus, the living one, we come with joy,
   truly, no evil can your love destroy.
   Teach us to walk in faith, though hope seems vain,
   reach out in love, we pray, renew again.

6. Jesus, the King of kings, we come to serve,
   freely give all for you as you deserve.
   Teach us to share the love you daily show,
   reach out in love, we pray, and bid us go.

TUNE 2: FARLEY CASTLE 10 10 10 10

1. Je - sus, the bro - ken bread, we come to you; emp - ty, we

would be fed – meet us a - new. Teach us to hun - ger af - ter

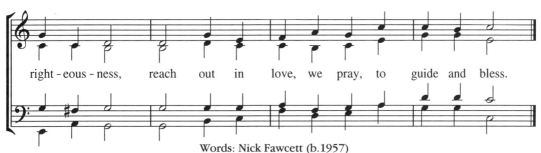

right - eous - ness, reach out in love, we pray, to guide and bless.

Words: Nick Fawcett (b.1957)
Music: Tune 1 – Noel Rawsthorne (b.1929)
Tune 2 – Henry Lawes (1596-1662)

37 Join the glorious celebration

MEN OF HARLECH 88 85 66 77 88 85

1. Join the glo-rious ce-le-bra-tion, with the God of re-cre-a-tion: ev-'ry race and ev-'ry na-tion, make a brand new start! Hear the peo-ple sing-ing! hear the gos-pel ring-ing: love for life, an end to strife, and truth e-ter-nal spring-ing. That's the hope, though

some des - pise it: God has pledged to re - a - lise it.

Raise the song to ad - ver - tise it: make a brand new start!

2. Round the world, the news is flying,
   where the hungry poor are dying,
   hear the voice of protest crying:
   'Make a brand new start!'
   God himself is calling,
   urgent and appalling!
   See his face
   in ev'ry place
   where tears of rage are falling:
   bring an end to exploitation,
   centuries of domination,
   break the chains that bind each nation:
   make a brand new start!

3. Praise the God who sought and found us
   when the chains of sin had bound us,
   spoke the words that still astound us:
   'Make a brand new start!'
   God of incarnation,
   be our inspiration;
   love be known
   and justice shown
   throughout your whole creation:
   earth and heav'n in Christ united,
   saints and sinners all invited,
   love resplendent, God delighted!
   Make a brand new start!

Words: Michael Forster (b.1946)
Music: traditional Welsh melody arr. Donald Thomson (b.1968)

38 Just one world

2. Just one word, holy word,
   here on earth, as our salvation,
   to help us live, live again,
   to live again through him.

Words and Music: Rick Wakeman (b.1949)

39 Let us rejoice

ENGLEBERG 10 10 10 4

1. Let us re - joice: God's gift to us is peace!

Here is the calm which bids our striv - ings cease,

for God's ac - cep - tance brings a true re - lease:

Vs. 1 to 4

al - le - lu - ia!

Last time

al - le - lu - ia!

2. We can be strong, for now we stand by grace,
held in his loving, fatherly embrace;
his care remains, whatever trials we face:
alleluia!

3. We trust in God, and shall not be dismayed,
nor find our hopes of glory are betrayed,
for all his splendour we shall see displayed:
alleluia!

4. And come what may, we never need despair –
God is at work through all the griefs we bear,
that in the end his likeness we may share:
alleluia!

5. Deep in our hearts the love of God is found;
his precious gifts of life and joy abound –
so let our finest songs of praise resound:
alleluia!

Words, based on Romans 5:1-5: Martin E. Leckebusch (b.1962)
Music: Charles Villiers Stanford (1852-1924)

40 Light a candle for thanksgiving!

TUNE 1: CANDLE 87 87 D

Unison

1. Light a can - dle for thanks - giv - ing! Sing to God for Christ the Lord! Born to Ma - ry, dy - ing, liv - ing; still the Spi - rit speaks his word. Wel - come ev - 'ry to - wer peal - ing, ce - le - brate two thou - sand years! Years of grace and years re - veal - ing Christ where Christ - like love ap - pears.

2. Light a candle for achievers!
   Marvel at their range of thought:
   artists, scientists, believers
   famed for what their hands have wrought.
   For the feats of engineering,
   for each fresh, creative probe;
   ev'ry benefit appearing,
   spread across a shrinking globe.

3. Light a candle for the nation
   and the future of its youth!
   Build with them on this foundation:
   love, security and truth.
   Christ the Lord, by patience winning
   many a household, many a heart,
   set ablaze their faith's beginning,
   journey with them from the start.

4. Light a candle for tomorrow!
   Ask that countries may walk free:
   truly free, not bound to borrow,
   but released for jubilee.
   One has come among us bearing
   news that prisoners are restored:
   let his voice move us to sharing –
   sing to God for Christ the Lord!

TUNE 2: HYFRYDOL 87 87 D

1. Light a can - dle for thanks - giv - ing! Sing to

God for Christ the Lord! Born to Ma - ry, dy - ing,

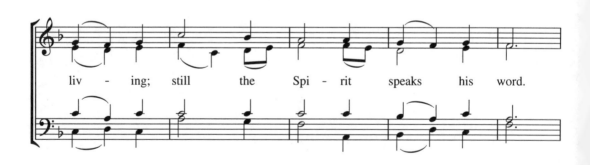

liv - ing; still the Spi - rit speaks his word.

Wel - come ev - 'ry to - wer peal - ing, ce - le - brate two

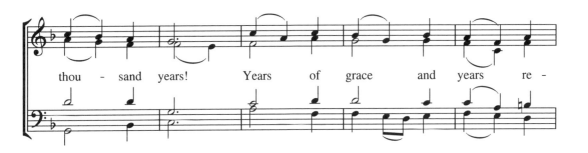

thou - sand years! Years of grace and years re -

veal - ing Christ where Christ - like love ap - pears.

2. Light a candle for achievers!
   Marvel at their range of thought:
   artists, scientists, believers
   famed for what their hands have wrought.
   For the feats of engineering,
   for each fresh, creative probe;
   ev'ry benefit appearing,
   spread across a shrinking globe.

3. Light a candle for the nation
   and the future of its youth!
   Build with them on this foundation:
   love, security and truth.
   Christ the Lord, by patience winning
   many a household, many a heart,
   set ablaze their faith's beginning,
   journey with them from the start.

4. Light a candle for tomorrow!
   Ask that countries may walk free:
   truly free, not bound to borrow,
   but released for jubilee.
   One has come among us bearing
   news that prisoners are restored:
   let his voice move us to sharing –
   sing to God for Christ the Lord!

Words: David Mowbray (b.1938)
Music: Tune 1 – Martin Setchell (b.1949)
Tune 2 – Rowland Huw Pritchard (1811-1887) arr. Ralph Vaughan Williams (1872-1958)

41 Living God, your word has called us

TUNE 1: TOR HILL 87 87 D

Unison

1. Liv - ing God, your word has called us, sum - moned us to
live by grace, make us one in hope and vi - sion,
as we ga - ther in this place. Take our search - ing,
take our prais - ing, take the si - lence of our prayer, of - fered up in
joy - ful wor - ship, spring - ing from the love we share.

2. Living God, your love has called us
   in the name of Christ your Son,
   forming us to be his body,
   by your Spirit making one.
   Working, laughing, learning, growing,
   old and young and black and white,
   gifts and skills together sharing,
   in your service all unite.

3. Living God, your hope has called us
   to the world that you have made,
   teaching us to live for others,
   humble, joyful, unafraid.
   Give us eyes to see your presence,
   joy in laughter, hope in pain.
   In our loving, in our living,
   give us strength that Christ may reign.

A lower setting of Tune 2 will be found at No. 47

TUNE 2: ABBOT'S LEIGH 87 87 D

1. Liv - ing God, your word has called us,
sum - moned us to live by grace,
make us one in hope and vi - sion,
as we ga - ther in this place.
Take our search - ing, take our prais - ing,

take the si - lence of our prayer,
of - fered up in joy - ful wor - ship,
spring - ing from the love we share.

2. Living God, your love has called us
   in the name of Christ your Son,
   forming us to be his body,
   by your Spirit making one.
   Working, laughing, learning, growing,
   old and young and black and white,
   gifts and skills together sharing,
   in your service all unite.

3. Living God, your hope has called us
   to the world that you have made,
   teaching us to live for others,
   humble, joyful, unafraid.
   Give us eyes to see your presence,
   joy in laughter, hope in pain.
   In our loving, in our living,
   give us strength that Christ may reign.

Words: Jan Berry (b.1953)
Music: Tune 1 – Malcolm Archer (b.1952)
Tune 2 – Cyril Vincent Taylor (1907-1991)

42 Living on the edge of destiny
Today, let this be the day

1. Liv - ing on the edge of des - ti - ny,
2. Break - ing through the haze of a - pa - thy,

look - ing in the face of pro - mi - ses;
dawns a new day of ex - pec - tan - cy;

we've ne - ver been this way be - fore, it could e - ven be to - day.

3. More than the pow - er of po - si - tive thought.

More than a rea - son to be - lieve. A

Words: Chris Bowater (b.1947)
Music: Chris Bowater (b.1947) arr. Donald Thomson (b.1968)

43 Lord, for the years

LORD OF THE YEARS 11 10 11 10

1. Lord, for the years your love has kept and gui-ded,
urged and in-spired us, cheered us on our way,
sought us and saved us, par-doned and pro-vi-ded,
Lord of the years, we bring our thanks to-day.

2. Lord, for that Word, the Word of life
   which fires us,
   speaks to our hearts and sets our souls ablaze,
   teaches and trains, rebukes us and inspires us,
   Lord of the Word, receive your people's praise.

3. Lord, for our land, in this our generation,
   spirits oppressed by pleasure, wealth and care;
   for young and old, for commonwealth and nation,
   Lord of our land, be pleased to hear our prayer.

4. Lord, for our world; when we disown
   and doubt him,
   loveless in strength, and comfortless in pain;
   hungry and helpless, lost indeed without him,
   Lord of the world, we pray that Christ may reign.

5. Lord, for ourselves; in living power remake us,
   self on the cross and Christ upon the throne;
   past put behind us, for the future take us,
   Lord of our lives, to live for Christ alone.

Words: Timothy Dudley-Smith (b.1926)
Music: Michael Baughen (b.1930) arr. David Iliff (b.1939)

44 Lord of all life and power

TUNE 1: COURT BARTON DSM

1. Lord of all life and power at whose cre - a - tive word in
na - ture's first pri - me - val hour our form-less be - ing stirred,
you made the light to shine, O shine on us, we pray, re -
new with light and life di - vine your church in this our day.

2. Lord of the fertile earth
who caused the world to be,
whose life alone can bring to birth
the fruits of land and sea,
teach us to use aright
and share the gifts you give,
to tend the earth as in your sight
that all the world may live.

3. Lord of the cross and grave
who died and lives again,
who came in love to seek and save
and then to rise and reign,
we share, as once you shared,
in mortal birth and breath,
and ours the risen life that dared
to vanquish sin and death.

4. Lord of the wind and flame,
   the promised Spirit's sign,
   possess our hearts in Jesus' name,
   come down, O Love divine!
   Help us in Christ to grow,
   from sin and self to cease,
   and daily in our lives to show
   your love and joy and peace.

5. Lord of the passing years
   whose changeless purpose stands,
   our lives and loves, our hopes and fears,
   we place within your hands;
   we bring you but your own,
   forgiven, loved and free,
   to follow Christ, and Christ alone,
   through all the days to be.

TUNE 2: DIADEMATA DSM

1. Lord of all life and power at whose cre-a-tive word in
na-ture's first pri-me-val hour our form-less be-ing stirred, you
made the light to shine, O shine on us, we pray, re-
new with light and life di-vine your church in this our day.

Words: Timothy Dudley-Smith (b.1926)
Music: Tune 1 – Malcolm Archer (b.1952)
Tune 2 – George Job Elvey (1816-1893)

45 Lord of all worlds

LORD OF THE YEARS 11 10 11 10

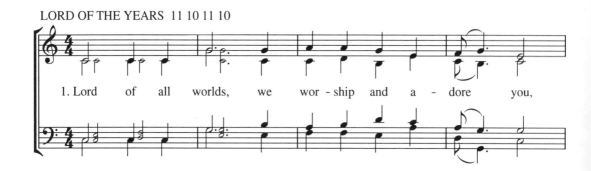

1. Lord of all worlds, we wor-ship and a-dore you,

cre-a-tion sings a gal-a-xy of praise:

the pla-nets fly, the stars cry out in won-der,

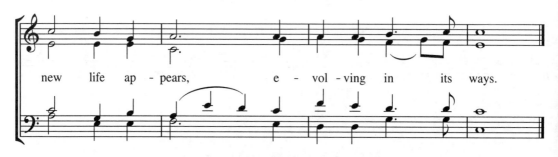

new life ap-pears, e-vol-ving in its ways.

2. You forged the sun, the molten light of morning;
   you scattered stars, flung jewels of the night;
   you are the day which penetrates our darkness:
   fill us with hope that we might share your light.

3. You summoned land from dark and heaving oceans,
   you moulded hills and carved the mountains high,
   you are the artist who is still creating:
   make us your partners lest the earth should die.

4. The glittering shoals flash through the rippling water,
   the gliding gull ascends the stream of air:
   now leaping thought and consecrated action
   become our way of living and of prayer.

5. You are the wind that rushes through the heavens,
   the breath that gently feeds us from our birth:
   we rest in you, our source and goal of living,
   we strive for you as stewards of your earth.

Words: Christopher Ellis (b.1949)
Music: Michael Baughen (b.1930) arr. David Iliff (b.1939)

46 Lord, we know that we have failed you

TUNE 1: WILLASTON 87 87 D

1. Lord, we know that we have failed you, false and fool-ish in so much, loath to lis-ten to your guid-ance, slow to re-cog-nise your touch. Though we keep you at a dis-tance, by our side, Lord, still re-main; cleanse our hearts, re-new our spi-rits, give us grace to start a-gain.

2. Lord, we know that we have failed you
through the things we do and say,
though we claim to care for others
we have thrust their needs away.
Too concerned with our own comfort
we have added to their pain;
teach us to show faith in action,
give us grace to start again.

3. Lord, we know that we have failed you,
full of doubt when life's been hard;
suffering has sapped our vision,
sorrow left our spirits scarred.
Faced by bitter disappointment
faith has buckled under strain;
help us know your hand upon us,
give us grace to start again.

4. Lord, we know that we have failed you,
   too familiar with your word,
   even though you've spoken clearly
   all too often we've not heard.
   Closed to truths which stretch horizons
   or which go against the grain –
   teach us, Lord, to stop and listen,
   give us grace to start again.

5. Lord, we know that we have failed you,
   lives too fraught to stop and stare;
   dwelling always on the present –
   what to eat or drink or wear.
   Teach us first to seek your kingdom,
   in our hearts for ever reign;
   send us out, restored, forgiven,
   give us grace to start again.

TUNE 2: EVERTON 87 87 D

1. Lord, we know that we have failed you, false and fool-ish in so much, loath to lis-ten to your guid-ance, slow to re-cog-nise your touch. Though we keep you at a dis-tance, by our side, Lord, still re-main; cleanse our hearts, re-new our spi-rits, give us grace to start a-gain.

Words: Nick Fawcett (b.1957)
Music: Tune 1 – Noel Rawsthorne (b.1929)
Tune 2 – Henry Smart (1813-1879)

47 Lord, we thank you for the promise

TUNE 1: THE PROMISE 87 87 D

1. Lord, we thank you for the pro - mise seen in ev - 'ry hu - man birth: you have planned each new be - gin - ning – who could hope for grea - ter worth? Hear our pray'r for those we che - rish; claim our child - ren as your own: in the fer - tile ground of child - hood may e - ter - nal seed

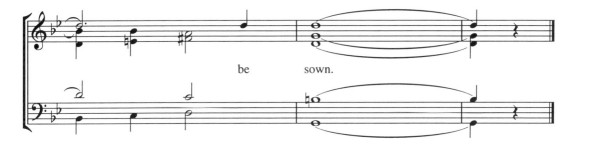

be sown.

2. Lord, we thank you for the vigour
   burning in the years of youth:
   strength to face tomorrow's challenge,
   zest for life and zeal for truth.
   In the choice of friends and partners,
   when ideas and values form,
   may the message of your kingdom
   be the guide, the goal, the norm.

3. Lord, we thank you for the harvest
   of the settled, middle years:
   times when work and home can prosper,
   when life's richest fruit appears;
   but when illness, stress and hardship
   fill so many days with dread,
   may your love renew the vision
   of a clearer road ahead.

4. Lord, we thank you for the beauty
   of a heart at last mature:
   crowned with peace and rich in wisdom,
   well-respected and secure;
   but to those who face the twilight
   frail, bewildered, lacking friends,
   Lord, confirm your gracious offer:
   perfect life which never ends.

A higher setting of Tune 2 will be found at No. 41

TUNE 2: ABBOT'S LEIGH 87 87 D

1. Lord, we thank you for the pro - mise

seen in ev - 'ry hu - man birth:

you have planned each new be - gin - ning –

who could hope for grea - ter worth?

Hear our pray'r for those we che - rish;

claim our chil - dren as your own:

in the fer - tile ground of child - hood

may e - ter - nal seed be sown.

2. Lord, we thank you for the vigour
   burning in the years of youth:
   strength to face tomorrow's challenge,
   zest for life and zeal for truth.
   In the choice of friends and partners,
   when ideas and values form,
   may the message of your kingdom
   be the guide, the goal, the norm.

3. Lord, we thank you for the harvest
   of the settled, middle years:
   times when work and home can prosper,
   when life's richest fruit appears;
   but when illness, stress and hardship
   fill so many days with dread,
   may your love renew the vision
   of a clearer road ahead.

4. Lord, we thank you for the beauty
   of a heart at last mature:
   crowned with peace and rich in wisdom,
   well-respected and secure;
   but to those who face the twilight
   frail, bewildered, lacking friends,
   Lord, confirm your gracious offer:
   perfect life which never ends.

Words: Martin E. Leckebusch (b.1962)
Music: Tune 1 – Martin Setchell (b.1949)
Tune 2 – Cyril Vincent Taylor (1907-1991)

48 May our breath be a song of praise

May our breath be a song of praise, may our lives be a sign of grace, may our words be an an - them raised to you. May our voice speak of vic - to - ry, may our hearts strive for u - ni - ty, may our deeds serve your ma - jes - ty, for

Words: P.J. Warren
Music: P.J. Warren arr. Donald Thomson (b.1968)

49 Name of all majesty

NAME OF ALL MAJESTY 66 64 D

1. Name of all ma-jes-ty, fa-thom-less mys-te-ry,

King of the a-ges by an-gels a-dored;

pow'r and au-tho-ri-ty, splen-dour and dig-ni-ty,

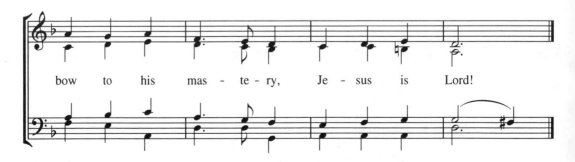

bow to his mas-te-ry, Je-sus is Lord!

2. Child of our destiny,
   God from eternity,
   Love of the Father
   on sinners outpoured;
   see now what God has done
   sending his only Son,
   Christ the beloved one,
   Jesus is Lord!

3. Saviour of Calvary,
   costliest victory,
   darkness defeated
   and Eden restored;
   born as a man to die,
   nailed to a cross on high,
   cold in the grave to lie,
   Jesus is Lord!

4. Source of all sovereignty,
   light, immortality,
   life everlasting
   and heaven assured;
   so with the ransomed, we
   praise him eternally,
   Christ in his majesty,
   Jesus is Lord!

Words: Timothy Dudley-Smith (b.1926)
Music: Malcolm Archer (b.1952)

50 New light has dawned

WEST ASHTON 10 10 10 10

Unison

1. New light has dawned, the Son of God is here, a
ho - ly light no earth - ly light out - shines; the
light has dawned, the light that casts out fear, the
light that e - vil dreads and love de - fines.

2. The light of glory shines to angels' song,
the shepherds run to where a baby lies;
a servant of the Lord, who waited long,
acclaims the light to lighten Gentile eyes.

3. And priestly men sit listening to a boy;
they see the dawning light within his face.
Such words they hear those Christ-child lips employ!
Amazing words of wisdom, truth and grace.

4. O Christ, the light who came to us on earth,
shine through the shadow cast by human sin;
renew the faith you gave at our new birth,
destroy the dark, and let your light come in.

WEST ASHTON 10 10 10 10

Harmony

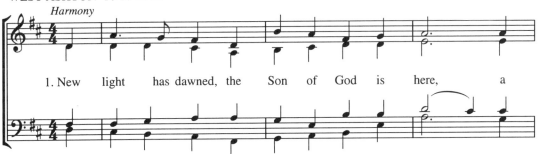

1. New light has dawned, the Son of God is here, a

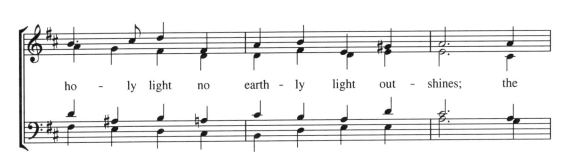

ho - ly light no earth - ly light out - shines; the

light has dawned, the light that casts out fear, the

light that e - vil dreads and love de - fines.

Words: Paul Wigmore (b.1925)
Music: John Barnard (b.1948)

51 No scenes of stately majesty

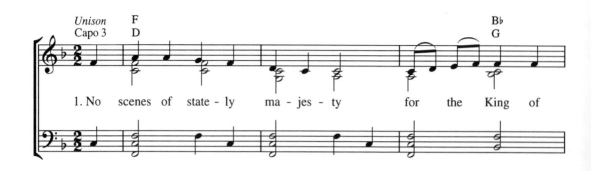

1. No scenes of state-ly ma-jes-ty for the King of

kings. No nights a-glow with can-dle flame for the King of

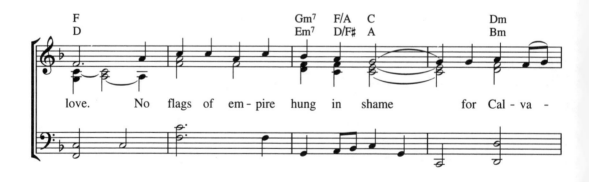

love. No flags of em-pire hung in shame for Cal-va-

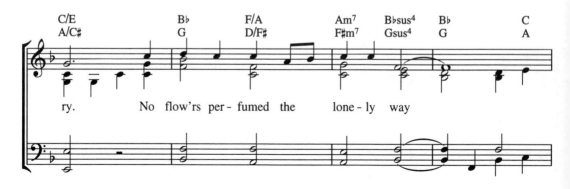

ry. No flow'rs per-fumed the lone-ly way

that led him to ... a bor-rowed tomb for Eas-ter Day.

2. No wreaths upon the ground were laid
   for the King of kings.
   Only a crown of thorns remained
   where he gave his love.
   A message scrawled in irony –
   King of the Jews –
   lay trampled where they turned away,
   and no one knew
   that it was the first Easter Day.

3. Yet nature's finest colours blaze
   for the King of kings.
   And stars in jewelled clusters say,
   'Worship heaven's King'.
   Two thousand springtimes more have bloomed –
   is that enough?
   Oh, how can I be satisfied
   until he hears
   the whole world sing of Easter love.

4. My prayers shall be a fragrance sweet
   for the King of kings.
   My love the flowers at his feet
   for the King of love.
   My vigil is to watch and pray
   until he comes.
   My highest tribute to obey
   and live to know
   the power of that first Easter Day.

5. I long for scenes of majesty
   for the risen King.
   For nights aglow with candle flame
   for the King of love.
   A nation hushed upon its knees
   at Calvary,
   where all our sins and griefs were nailed
   and hope was born
   of everlasting Easter Day.

Words and Music: Graham Kendrick (b.1950)

52 O God, enthroned in majesty

HOLFORD 86 86 D

1. O God, en-throned in ma - jes-ty and crowned with mor - tal pain, in - spired by your a - maz - ing love we turn to you a - gain; for grace and judge - ment here com - bine to meet our deep - est need, no cheap and ea - sy for - mu - la, but cost - ly grace, in - deed!

2. Confronted by the awesome truth,
   we shrink away in fear:
   all sin is death, the cross proclaims,
   and none stands blameless here.
   Yet through the pain, amazing love
   assures us of your grace,
   and gives us courage to return
   and stand before your face.

3. Now give us grace to stand beneath
   the crosses of the world,
   that all may judge the power of sin,
   yet see your love unfurled.
   Let no more lives be crucified
   by poverty or war,
   but grace and judgement, hand in hand,
   unite to cry, 'No more!'

4. Then let the world be freed from fear
   to seek love's open way,
   to journey from untimely night
   toward a greater day:
   to justice, hope and liberty,
   the kingdom of your choice,
   when all our praise is gathered up
   in one united voice.

Words: Michael Forster (b.1946)
Music: John Marsh (b.1939)

53 O God of hope

REPTON 86 88 6

1. O God of hope, your pro - phets spoke of days when war would cease: when, taught to see each per - son's worth, and faith - ful stew - ards of the earth, we all would live in peace, we all would live in peace.

2. We pray that our divided world
   may hear their words anew:
   then lift for good the curse of war,
   let bread with justice bless the poor,
   and turn in hope to you.

3. Earth's fragile web of life demands
   our reverence and our care,
   lest in our folly, sloth and greed,
   deaf both to you and others' need,
   we lay our planet bare.

4. Earth's rich resources give us power
   to build or to destroy:
   your Spirit urges us to turn
   from selfish, fear-bound ways, and learn
   his selfless trust and joy.

5. The Prince of Peace is calling us
   to shun the way of strife:
   he brings us healing through his pain;
   our shattered hope is born again
   through his victorious life.

Words: Basil E. Bridge (b.1927)
Music: Charles Hubert Hastings Parry (1848-1918)

54 O Lord, our hope in every generation

HIGHWOOD 11 10 11 10

1. O Lord, our hope in ev-'ry ge - ne - ra - tion, you reigned be - fore the u - ni - verse be - gan: we bear your i - mage, we are your cre - a - tion; and yet how frail we are, how brief life's span.

2. A thousand years like yesterday in passing,
   or like the waking memory of our dreams,
   like plants that flower at noon but die by evening,
   so, Lord, to you our transient glory seems.

3. O Holy Lord, forgive our self-deceiving;
   our secret sins are clear before your face;
   free us to share the joy of those believing
   they are restored by your eternal grace.

4. Time rushes by: we need your gift of wisdom
   to know your will and follow your commands;
   yours is the power, the glory and the kingdom;
   work out your timeless purpose through our hands.

Words, based on Psalm 90: Basil E. Bridge (b.1927)
Music: Richard Runciman Terry (1865-1938)

55 Open our eyes

TUNE 1: BROMBOROUGH 12 12 8 8

With breadth

mf *legato*

Unison

1. O - pen our eyes to see the an - guish of the poor –

in - dig - ni - ties un - told where life is

in - se - cure; then may our ears dis - cern your

call to de - mon - strate your care for all.

3. O - pen our hands to give, to serve through all our deeds,

and let our strength be spent to meet our

neigh- bours' needs; let love, not du – ty, be our

guide: Lord, let our hearts be o – pen wide!

TUNE 2: LOVE UNKNOWN 66 66 44 44

1. O - pen our eyes to see the an - guish of the
poor – in - dig - ni - ties un - told where life is
in - se - cure; then may our ears dis -
cern your call to de - mon - strate your care for all.

2. Open our minds to grasp
   life's grim reality –
   how greed and power prolong
   the curse of poverty;
   and fill our mouths with words to speak,
   defending those whose voice is weak.

3. Open our hands to give,
   to serve through all our deeds,
   and let our strength be spent
   to meet our neighbours' needs;
   let love, not duty, be our guide:
   Lord, let our hearts be open wide!

Words: Martin E. Leckebusch (b.1962)
Music: Tune 1 – Noel Rawsthorne (b.1929)
Tune 2 – John Ireland (1879-1962)

56 Overflow with joy and gladness

TUNE 1: SPELTHORNE 87 87 D

1. O - ver - flow with joy and glad - ness, sing, my soul, for free - dom gained; God has wiped a - way our sad - ness and the pris - 'ners are un - chained. Gone the an - guish, gone the sor - row, gone the ma - na - cles of fear; faith has tri - umphed, and to - mor - row shines with sun - light, bright and clear.

2. Those whose hope is in their Saviour,
   those who trust in Christ their Lord,
   now proclaim by their behaviour
   inward peace and true accord.
   Like believers of past ages,
   who for Jesus Christ were bold,
   from such martyrs, saints and sages
   no good thing does God withhold.

3. So, in gratitude, before you,
   God our Father, sun and shield,
   full of praises, we adore you,
   as the powers of darkness yield.
   For this mighty liberation,
   after grief and torment long,
   we rejoice in your salvation:
   hear, O God, our triumph song!

A higher setting of Tune 2 will be found at No. 10

TUNE 2: ODE TO JOY 87 87 D

1. O - ver - flow with joy and glad - ness, sing, my soul, for free - dom gained;

God has wiped a - way our sad - ness and the pris - 'ners are un - chained.

Gone the an - guish, gone the sor - row, gone the ma - na - cles of fear;

faith has tri - umphed, and to - mor - row shines with sun - light, bright and clear.

Words: Michael Saward (b.1932)
Music: Tune 1 – Brian Hoare (b.1935)
Tune 2 – Ludwig van Beethoven (1770-1827) arr. Christopher Tambling (b.1964)

57 Praise the Lord of heaven

VICARS' CLOSE 76 76 D

1. Praise the Lord of hea-ven, praise him in the height;
praise him, all his an-gels, praise him, hosts of light.
Sun and moon to-ge-ther, shi-ning stars a-flame,
pla-nets in their cour-ses, mag-ni-fy his name!

2. Earth and ocean praise him;
mountains, hills and trees;
fire and hail and tempest,
wind and storm and seas.
Praise him, fields and forests,
birds on flashing wings,
praise him, beasts and cattle,
all created things.

3. Now by prince and people
let his praise be told;
praise him, men and maidens,
praise him, young and old.
He, the Lord of glory!
We, his praise proclaim!
High above all heavens
magnify his name!

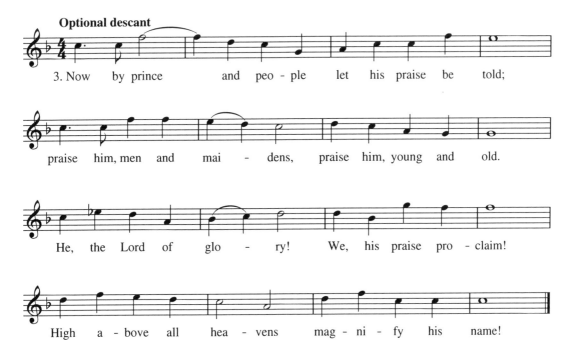

Optional descant

3. Now by prince and peo - ple let his praise be told;

praise him, men and mai - dens, praise him, young and old.

He, the Lord of glo - ry! We, his praise pro - claim!

High a - bove all hea - vens mag - ni - fy his name!

Words, based on Psalm 148: Timothy Dudley-Smith (b.1926)
Music: Malcolm Archer (b.1952)

58 Silently at Christmas

TUNE 1: THIS MORN Irregular

1. Si - lent - ly at Christ - mas Je - sus came to town, home-less -ness he suf - fered, in a sta - ble born. Son of God al - migh - ty, heir to hea - ven's crown, pow'r -less -ness he suf - fered on that morn.

2. Hurriedly at Christmas
   shepherds came to town,
   guilelessness they offered,
   in the humble barn.
   To the Lord almighty,
   heir to heaven's crown,
   lowliness they offered
   on that morn.

3. Painfully at Christmas
   people live in town,
   hopelessness they suffer
   hungry and alone.
   Cursing the almighty
   heir to heaven's crown,
   thoughtlessness they suffer
   on this morn.

4. Willingly at Christmas,
   Christians in our town,
   joyfulness they offer,
   carolling the Son,
   and to Christ almighty,
   heir to heaven's crown,
   selflessness they offer
   on this morn.

5. Longingly each Christmas
   Jesus comes to town,
   godlessness he suffers,
   how his heart must burn!
   He is love almighty,
   heir to heaven's crown,
   loneliness he suffers
   on this morn.

TUNE 2: CRANHAM Irregular

1. Silently at Christmas Jesus came to town, homelessness he suffered, in a stable born. Son of God almighty, heir to heaven's crown, pow'rlessness he suffered on that morn.

Words: Michael Saward (b.1932)
Music: Tune 1 – Andrew Wright (b.1955)
Tune 2 – Gustav Holst (1874-1934)

59 Sing glory to God the Father

TE DEUM 8 12 8 8 8 13 13

1. Sing glo-ry to God the Fa - ther, the King of the u - ni - verse, change-less-ly the same. Sing praise to the world's cre - a - tor and mag - ni - fy his ho - ly name. He made all that is round us and all that is be - yond, his hands up - hold the pla - nets, to him they all res - pond.

Fine

D.C.

2. Sing glory to God the Saviour,
   the Lord of the galaxies, bearer of our shame.
   Sing praise to the world's redeemer
   and magnify his holy name.

   He suffered grief and torment, for sin he paid the price,
   he rose in glorious triumph, both priest and sacrifice.

3. Sing glory to God the Spirit,
   the power of the elements, setting hearts aflame.
   Sing praise to the world's life-giver
   and magnify his holy name.

   His gifts to all are given, his fruit transforms our hearts,
   his fellowship enriches, a grace which he imparts.

4. Sing glory, the whole creation!
   Give thanks to the Trinity, heaven's love proclaim.
   Sing praise to our God, almighty,
   and magnify his holy name.

Words: Michael Saward (b.1932)
Music: Marc-Antoine Charpentier (1634-1704)
adapted and arranged by Donald Thomson (b.1968)

60 Stars: shine!

HAZELWOOD Irregular

Stars: shine! Bells: chime! An - gels: tell us that it's

real - ly true. God is in his world, and his world is new.

1. Come, let us meet at the man - ger, learn from the child who is

born. New life be - gins at the man - ger,

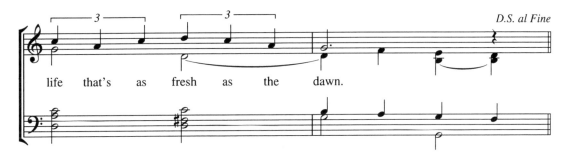

life   that's   as   fresh   as   the   dawn.

2. Families meet at the manger,
   learn from the child who is Word.
   New life begins at the manger,
   life where all voices are heard.

3. Governments meet at the manger,
   learn from the child who is Lord.
   New life begins at the manger,
   life that is free from the sword.

4. Come, let us meet at the manger,
   learn from the child who is Love.
   New life begins at the manger,
   life as a gift from above.

Words: Michael Forster (b.1946)
Music: Richard Lloyd (b.1933)

NewStart Hymns and Songs

61 Take my hands, Lord
Take my life

2. Give me someone to feed when I'm hungry,
   when I'm thirsty, give water for their thirst.
   When I stand in need of tenderness,
   give me someone to hold who longs for love.

3. Keep my heart ever open to others,
   may my time, Lord, be spent with those in need;
   may I tend to those who need your care.
   Take my life, Lord, and make it truly yours.

Words: verses 1 & 3 Margaret Rizza (b.1929); verse 2 unknown
Music: Margaret Rizza (b.1929)

62 Take my heart

SELWYN COLLEGE 11 11 11 8

1. Take my heart, Lord God of my cre - a - tion,

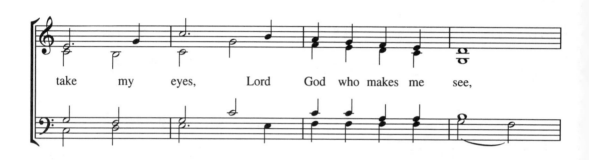

take my eyes, Lord God who makes me see,

take my mind, Lord God who makes me wor - ship;

to be your ser - vant, Lord; take me.

2. Take my strength, Lord God of dedication,
   take my anger, Lord who calmed the sea,
   take my love, Lord God who came to love me;
   to be your stronghold, Lord; take me.

3. Take my thoughts, Lord God of inspiration,
   take my hands, take my humanity,
   take my friends, Lord God who shared your friendship;
   for your companion, Lord; take me.

4. Take my path, Lord God of inspiration,
   take my sins, Lord God who sets me free,
   take my soul, Lord God who knows my weakness;
   to be your pilgrim, Lord; take me.

5. Take my life, Lord God of resurrection,
   take my all, Lord God who holds the key,
   take my heart, Lord God whose heart was broken;
   for your disciple, Lord; take me.

Words and Music: Andrew Gant (b.1963)

63 Thanks be to God

SONG 46 10 10

1. Thanks be to God for his most ho - ly

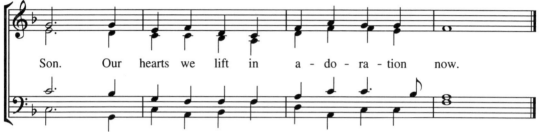

Son. Our hearts we lift in a - do - ra - tion now.

2. Thanks be to God
   for all the Spirit's power.
   Our hearts we lift
   in liberation now.

3. Thanks be to God
   for giving us new birth.
   Our hearts we lift
   in consecration now.

4. Thanks be to God
   for eucharistic food.
   Our hearts we lift
   in exultation now.

5. Thanks be to God
   for hope of heaven's joy.
   Our hearts we lift
   in expectation now.

6. Thanks be to God,
   blessed Trinity above.
   Our hearts we lift
   in veneration now.

Words: Michael Saward (b.1932)
Music: Orlando Gibbons (1583-1625)

64 The kingdom of the living God

KINGDOM 86 86 86

1. The king-dom of the liv-ing God has come, as Christ pro-claimed; for he, the King, has, on his throne the hu-man heart re-claimed, when, crowned with thorns, up-on the cross, his king-ship has been named.

2. In action and in parable
   that kingdom has been taught.
   Its character, transforming lives,
   is by disciples sought;
   for Jesus, with the blood he shed,
   has our salvation bought.

3. This King has our allegiance won,
   our lives to him are bound,
   he calls us as his royal priests
   to treat as holy ground
   the whole wide world for which he died
   and rose, and now is crowned.

4. And yet we pray, 'Your kingdom come',
   that holy city bright,
   for he who came a peasant babe
   shall come in radiant light
   to bring that kingdom here on earth
   and reign in glorious might.

Words: Michael Saward (b.1932)
Music: Malcolm Archer (b.1952)

65 The road through life

1. The road through life, the road is long and hard, O Lord, my feet are wea-ry and sore; the go-ing's rough and things are get-ting tough, but, Lord, I know you've gone be - fore.

Refrain

Roads, Lord, roads, Lord, how hard my road can be,

2. The map of life is not too clear to read,
   and I get lost on many a day;
   the going's rough and things are getting tough,
   but, Lord, I know you know the way.

3. Sometimes ahead the road is black as night
   and ev'ry step is full of fear;
   the going's rough and things are getting tough,
   but, Lord, I know that you are here.

Words: June L. Baker (b.1936)
Music: June L. Baker (b.1936) arr. Donald Thomson (b.1968)

66 The universe was waiting

TUNE 1: DORE ABBEY 76 76 D

1. The u-ni-verse was wait-ing in dark cha-o-tic night, un-til the word was spo-ken: 'Let there be glo-rious light!' From dark-ness and from cha-os were light and or-der born; the God of new be-gin-nings re-joiced to see their dawn.

2. And as in that beginning,
in every age the same,
creation's Re-creator
is keeping hope aflame.
From Eden to the desert,
the manger to the tomb,
each fall becomes a rising,
and every grave a womb.

3. Wherever people languish
in darkness or despair,
the God of new beginnings
is pierced, and rises there.
We join with him, to listen,
to care, and to protest,
to see the mighty humbled
and all the humble blessed.

4. We join with our Creator
to keep the vision bright:
in places of oppression
we call for freedom's light:
a glorious new beginning,
a universe at peace,
where justice flows like fountains
and praises never cease.

TUNE 2: THORNBURY 76 76 D

1. The u- ni-verse was wait - ing in dark, cha - o - tic night, un - til the word was spo - ken: 'Let there be glo - rious light!' From dark -ness and from cha - os were light and or - der born; the God of new be - gin - nings re -

Unison

joiced to see their dawn.

Words: Michael Forster (b.1946)
Music: Tune 1 – Alan Rees (b.1941); Tune 2 – Basil Harwood (1859-1949)

67 This is the time of celebration

1. This is the time of ce - le - bra - tion.
This is the sea - son of great joy.
All o - ver the world God's Spi - rit is mov - ing.

2. Two thousand years since his coming
   Jesus still calls us to share his love.
   With voices that speak for truth and justice,
   offering hope to everyone.

3. Spread the Good News of God's compassion.
   Lift up your eyes with faith and prayer.
   The fields are now ready for the harvest.
   Go tell the people everywhere.

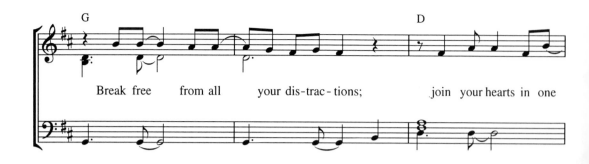

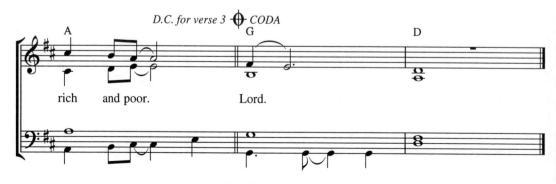

Words: Dave Bilbrough
Music: Dave Bilbrough arr. Donald Thomson (b.1968)

New**Start** Hymns and Songs

68 Through days of rage and wonder

still are the bread and wine:

our hope a cross that tow - ers

o - ver the wrecks of time.

D.C.
(Fine)

3. Through days of rage and wonder,
   by the awesome power of prayer
   God will shake every nation,
   secrets will be laid bare.
   And if his light increasing
   casts deeper shadows here,
   safe in his holy presence,
   love will cast out our fear.

4. Through days of rage and wonder
   you will give us strength to stand
   and seek a heavenly city
   not built by human hands.
   Now is the only moment
   within our power to change:
   to give back in obedience
   while life and breath remain.

Words: Graham Kendrick (b.1950)
Music: Graham Kendrick (b.1950) arr. Donald Thomson (b.1968)

69 Two thousand years since Bethlehem

TUNE 1: PENTON HOOK DCM

1. Two thou-sand years since Beth-le-hem first wel-comed Je-sus' birth: the start-ling truth be-gan to dawn that God had come to earth. And as he grew and lived and taught a diff-'rent way un-furled: a way of joy and love and peace,

To verses

a new start for the world!

Last time

chance to start a - gain!

2. Two thousand years since Galilee
   where Jesus preached and healed;
   in words of truth and works of power
   God's kingdom was revealed.
   As young and old and rich and poor
   responded to his call,
   they found what we may find today:
   a new start for us all!

3. Two thousand years since Calvary,
   the hill where Jesus died;
   the Lamb of God, the sinless one,
   for me was crucified.
   But soon he rose up from the grave
   to reign in victory;
   good news I scarcely can believe:
   a new start won for me!

4. Two thousand years since Pentecost:
   the Holy Spirit came
   in sound of mighty, rushing wind
   and tongues of living flame;
   a gift to all who will believe
   and live the Jesus way;
   the power of God we may receive,
   a new start from today!

5. Two thousand years of Christian faith
   have changed our history,
   for Jesus is the Lord of time
   and of eternity.
   For all who seek a better way,
   than failure, sin and pain,
   still Jesus Christ makes all things new:
   a chance to start again!

TUNE 2: KINGSFOLD DCM

1. Two thou-sand years since Beth-le-hem first wel-comed Je-sus'

birth: the start-ling truth be-gan to dawn that

God had come to earth. And as he grew and

lived and taught a diff-'rent way un - furled: a

way of joy and love and peace, a new start for the world!

2. Two thousand years since Galilee
   where Jesus preached and healed;
   in words of truth and works of power
   God's kingdom was revealed.
   As young and old and rich and poor
   responded to his call,
   they found what we may find today:
   a new start for us all.

3. Two thousand years since Calvary,
   the hill where Jesus died;
   the Lamb of God, the sinless one,
   for me was crucified.
   But soon he rose up from the grave
   to reign in victory;
   good news I scarcely can believe:
   a new start won for me!

4. Two thousand years since Pentecost:
   the Holy Spirit came
   in sound of mighty, rushing wind
   and tongues of living flame;
   a gift to all who will believe
   and live the Jesus way;
   the power of God we may receive,
   a new start from today!

5. Two thousand years of Christian faith
   have changed our history,
   for Jesus is the Lord of time
   and of eternity.
   For all who seek a better way,
   than failure, sin and pain,
   still Jesus Christ makes all things new:
   a chance to start again!

Words: Brian Hoare (b.1935)
Music: Tune 1 – Brian Hoare (b.1935)
Tune 2 – traditional English melody adapted and arranged by Ralph Vaughan Williams (1872-1958)

70 Warm as the sun

TUNE 1: WARM AS THE SUN LM

so un - to me, Lord, is your love.

Je - sus, for you, such is my love, Je - sus, for you.

2. Lovely as dawn, welcome as light,
   peaceful as dusk, restful as night,
   high as the clouds, deep as the sea,
   so is your love, Lord, unto me.

3. Swift as a stream, free as a bird,
   firm as a rock, sure as your word,
   bright as the stars, shining above,
   so unto me, Lord, is your love.

4. Finer than silk, richer than money,
   precious as gold, sweeter than honey,
   priceless as jewels, dear as can be,
   so is your love, Lord, unto me.

5. Bursting with joy, leaping with praise,
   glowing with thanks, heart set ablaze;
   bringing my life, all that I do,
   such is my love, Jesus, for you.

TUNE 2: O WALY WALY LM

1. Warm as the sun, fresh as the breeze, fair as a

flower, tall as the trees, clear as the dew, pure as the

To verses 2 to 4

dove, so un-to me, Lord, is your love. 2. Love-ly as

To verse 5

me. 5. Burst-ing with joy, leap-ing with praise, glow-ing with

thanks, heart set a - blaze; bring-ing my life, all that I

do, such is my love, Je - sus, for you.

2. Lovely as dawn, welcome as light,
   peaceful as dusk, restful as night,
   high as the clouds, deep as the sea,
   so is your love, Lord, unto me.

3. Swift as a stream, free as a bird,
   firm as a rock, sure as your word,
   bright as the stars, shining above,
   so unto me, Lord, is your love.

4. Finer than silk, richer than money,
   precious as gold, sweeter than honey,
   priceless as jewels, dear as can be,
   so is your love, Lord, unto me.

5. Bursting with joy, leaping with praise,
   glowing with thanks, heart set ablaze;
   bringing my life, all that I do,
   such is my love, Jesus, for you.

Words: Nick Fawcett (b.1957)
Music: Tune 1 – Margaret Rizza (b.1929)
Tune 2 – Somerset folk song collected by Cecil Sharp (1859-1924) arr. Richard Lloyd (b.1933)

71 We shall see him in the morning

TUNE 1: NESTON 87 87

Tranquillo   *Unison*

legato   1. We shall see him in the morning when the mists of life have cleared, with his arms out-stretched to greet us from a jour-ney we had feared.

Men 2. Those who toiled all night and struggled
till the earthly fight was won
will awaken to the music
of his welcoming 'Well done!'

Women 3. We shall recognise the Master
with his wounded hands and side
as we worship him, the glorious,
the ascended Crucified.

4. Though the shore now seems so distant
we await the morning light
and the breakfast celebration
when our faith gives way to sight.

TUNE 2: ALL FOR JESUS 87 87

1. We shall see him in the morn-ing when the mists of life have cleared,

with his arms out-stretched to greet us from a jour-ney we have feared.

Words: Randle Manwaring (b.1912)
Music: Tune 1 – Noel Rawsthorne (b.1929)
Tune 2 – John Stainer (1840-1901)

72 What shall we bring

TUNE 1: WORTLEY 10 10 10 10 and Refrain

1. What shall we bring to give hon - our to God:
wor - ship and sac - ri - fice, pray - ing and song?
This is all no - thing un - less we can bring
jus - tice and mer - cy to hon - our our King.

Walk with our God, hum - bly each

day. Help us to do all that we say. Jus - tice and mer - cy should crown all we bring – this is the wor - ship we of - fer our King.

2. Save us, O Lord, from the hypocrite's prayer:
   bringing you praise while our deeds are unfair.
   help us to honour all people on earth:
   each one is precious, of infinite worth.

3. Save us, O Lord, from excuse and neglect,
   show us the world as you see it today.
   Kindle within us a passion for good;
   give us the strength to do all that we should.

TUNE 2: THE GLORY SONG 10 10 10 10 and Refrain

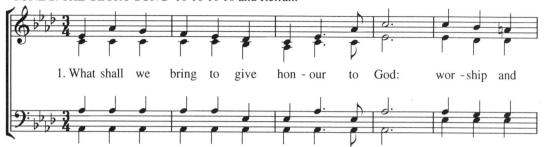

1. What shall we bring to give hon - our to God: wor -ship and

sac - ri - fice, pray-ing and song? This is all no - thing un -

less we can bring jus - tice and mer - cy to hon - our our

Refrain

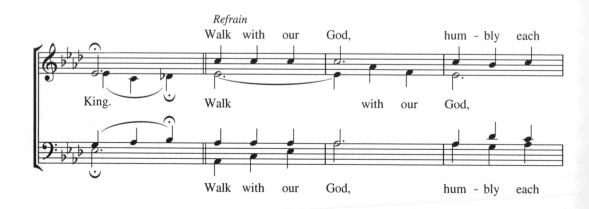

King. Walk with our God,
Walk with our God, hum - bly each

Walk with our God, hum - bly each

2. Save us, O Lord, from the hypocrite's prayer:
   bringing you praise while our deeds are unfair.
   help us to honour all people on earth:
   each one is precious, of infinite worth.

3. Save us, O Lord, from excuse and neglect,
   show us the world as you see it today.
   Kindle within us a passion for good;
   give us the strength to do all that we should.

Words, based on Micah 6:6-8: Christopher Ellis (b.1949)
Music: Tune 1 – Richard Lloyd (b.1933)
Tune 2 – C.H. Gabriel (1856-1932)

Indexes

Index of Authors

Index of Composers, Arrangers and Sources of Music

Alphabetical Index of Tunes

Metrical Index of Tunes

Thematic Index

The hymns and songs in this collection were written to focus particularly on the themes chosen for the Millennium. These themes are:

A New Start for the World's Poor
A New Start at Home
A New Start with God

Scriptural Index

Index of First Lines and Titles

This index gives the first line of each hymn. If a hymn is known by an alternative title, this is also given, but indented and in italics.